Cañons Grandé

VISIONS of the GRAND STAIRCASE

A WISH YOU WERE HERE® BOOK

BY
LYNN WILSON, JIM WILSON
AND
JEFF NICHOLAS

SIERRA PRESS, INC.

ISBN 0-939365-09-X (Paper)
0-939365-18-9 (Cloth)

Printed in Hong Kong
First Edition

ACKNOWLEDGEMENTS

We wish to thank Ellis Richard of Grand Canyon, Tim Manns of Zion and Edd Franz of Bryce Canyon, as well as the dedicated interpretive and Natural History Association staffs, both past and present, of each Park on the Grand Staircase. It is due to their foresight and hard work that wonderlands such as these are still here for each of us to enjoy. It is up to each of us, as individuals, to make certain our own use is consistent with the long-term needs of these natural temples.

SIERRA PRESS, INC.

P.O. BOX 430, EL PORTAL, CA. 95318

DEDICATION

*This book is dedicated
to those who stop;*

to see, to hear, to smell, to taste, to feel,

*not just to know,
but to understand.*

CONTENTS

INTRODUCTION   4
GRAND CANYON   6
ZION   28
BRYCE CANYON   58
NEARBY GEMS   78
STAIRCASE NOTES   90

INTRODUCTION

Just what, you ask, is this Grand Staircase?

It is the Grand Canyon, it is Zion, it is Bryce. It is the sum total of all the land surrounding them. It is Coral Pink Sand Dunes and Kodachrome Basin. It is Cedar Breaks and cliffs called chocolate, vermilion, grey, white and pink.

It is hot, sun-blasted sandstone and it is forests of aspen, spruce and fir.

It is a million acres of scorched earth and luxuriant hanging gardens.

It is a land of ear-shattering silence. It is the roar of

It is columbines dancing on the breeze, rattle-snakes buzzing among the rocks.

It is a land of buttes, mesas and plateaus; of spires, pinnacles and towers; of cañons, arroyos and ravines; of arches, windows and bridges.

It is a land of 100-mile-horizons and blood-red chasms so deep and twisted that they appear bathed in twilight at midday.

It is howling spring gales, gentle summer breezes and the hushed stillness of a winter morn.

It is Zen-like simplicity. It is Wagnerian opulence.

It is ravens flying wing tip to wing tip with their own shadows, and it is bighorns gliding across

It is as new and fresh as spring wildflowers and it is older than life on earth.

It is the crunch of gravel underfoot and the heart-stopping miracle of fresh mountain lion tracks in the sand of perennial streams.

It is still quaint Mormon towns, ancient cities of stone and 500-million-year-old fossils.

It is Wotan's Throne, Furnace Flats and Buddha's Temple; it is Thor's Hammer, Towers of the Virgin, Molly's Nipple and the Tropic Ditch. It is Rock Rovers Land, Sipupani and a helluva place to lose a cow.

It is the blinding light of noon in mid-summer and the warming embrace of a winter sunset.

It is the music of dripping water and the rumble of distant rock falls.

It is turquoise pools of potholed rainwater and the foaming red rage of liquid mud.

It is the heart-lifting song of the canyon wren and the laughing of ravens.

It is juniper, pine, and sage; spruce, locoweed and aspen; microbiotic soil, prickly pear and bladderpod; cottonwood, primrose and sacred datura.

It has been called a "profitless locality" in an "altogether valueless" region and it is "the most sublime spectacle on earth".

It is a land that will wear you out, tear you down and leave you for the vultures. A land that will fill your being, lift your spirit and make your life worth fighting for.

All of that is what the Grand Staircase is.

Grand Canyon

Rise up. Rise up. Oh eye of day,
Shine deep, deep within.
Give lift to the morning fog
And song to the canyon wren.

Illuminate the spider web
with tiny prismed dew.
Illuminate the rainbow,
Cloud tears passing through.

Illuminate the paths of man,
From Supapuni's hole,
Tracing each achievement,
And every earthly goal.

Illuminate the walls of stone,
Earth's history written on.
Or perhaps it's this empty void,
That carries history gone?

Is it the vast nothing,
That's confounding 'bout this place?
The forever wide, the forever deep,
The forever empty space?

Maybe it's the lizard,
As he slips across the earth?
Or possibly a cactus bud,
As it prepares for birth?

Is it in the cottonwoods,
Shedding leaves in Autumn?
Or is it in the tiny bird,
That walks the river bottom?

i hear it in the raven's cry,
As it soars beneath the rim.
i feel it in the prick of yucca,
As it harshly breaks my skin.

i smell it in the air,
As it breathes across this land.
i taste it in the water,
As it flows from ancient sand.

i see it in the paintings,
Of those who've come before.
i know that it is all these things,
That open wisdom's door.

This land makes me think!

SUNSET AND RAINBOW, MATHER POINT

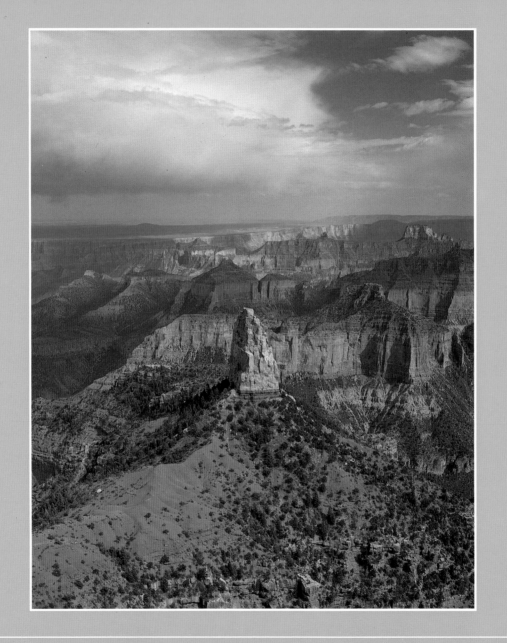

MT. HAYDEN, POINT IMPERIAL

SUNRISE, WOTAN'S THRONE

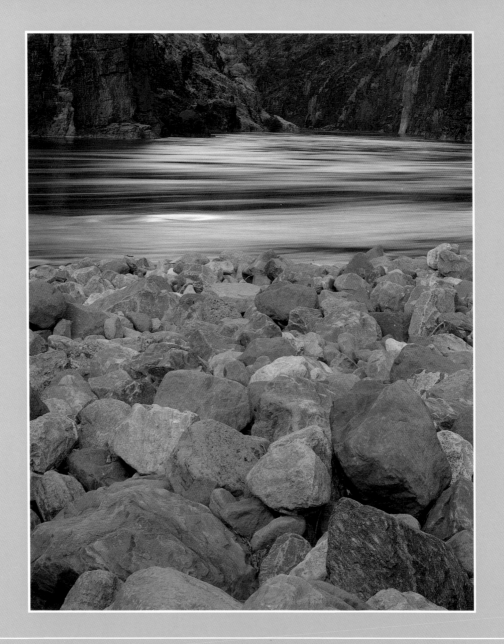

GRANITE GORGE AT GRANITE RAPIDS

PAINTBRUSH AND YUCCA

VIEW FROM BRIGHT ANGEL LODGE

SUNSET FROM POWELL MEMORIAL

ANGEL'S WINDOW, NORTH RIM

FALL ASPENS, NORTH RIM

COLORADO RIVER AT MONUMENT CREEK

FRESH SNOW AT MORNING, SOUTH RIM

22

ROYAL ARCH CREEK

PLUNGE POOL, OLO CANYON

MOHAVE WALL, WINTER

DEER CREEK, INNER CANYON

RAINBOW OVER THE COLORADO RIVER, FURNACE FLATS

Zion

WEST TEMPLE AND TOWERS OF THE VIRGIN

Eons of time.
A million, million grains of sand.
A thousand rippled layers.
A hundred moods of light.
Countless shades of red

And green.

Sand to rock.
Rock to sand.
Swirled, etched, gouged and grooved.
Dolloped to resemble petrified meringue.
Cut to a valley with river

And green.

Red and green. Red and green. Red and green.
Clouds dance across the blue.
Shadows dance across the red

And green.

This land makes me humble!

GREAT WHITE THRONE, AUTUMN

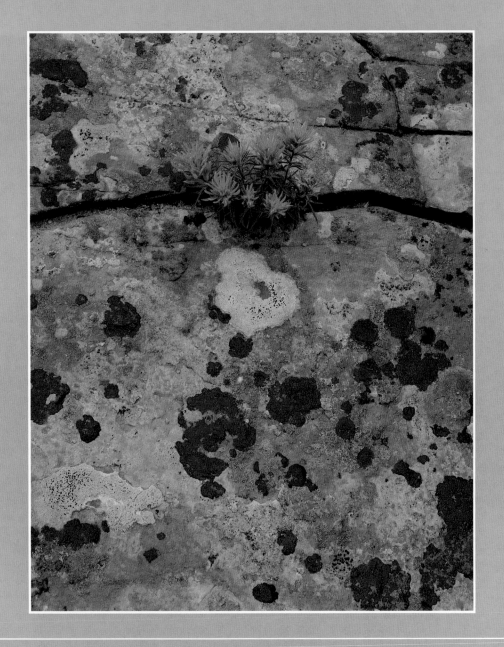

PAINTBRUSH AND LICHENS

PINE AND CROSSBEDDED SANDSTONE

32

SNOW AND SANDSTONE WALL

WINTER REFLECTIONS, TEMPLE OF SINAWAVA

CROSSBEDDED SANDSTONE, HIGH COUNTRY

VALLEY OF THE VIRGIN RIVER, ZION CANYON

THE PULPIT

RAINBOW OVER ZION CANYON

INSIDE DOUBLE ARCH ALCOVE

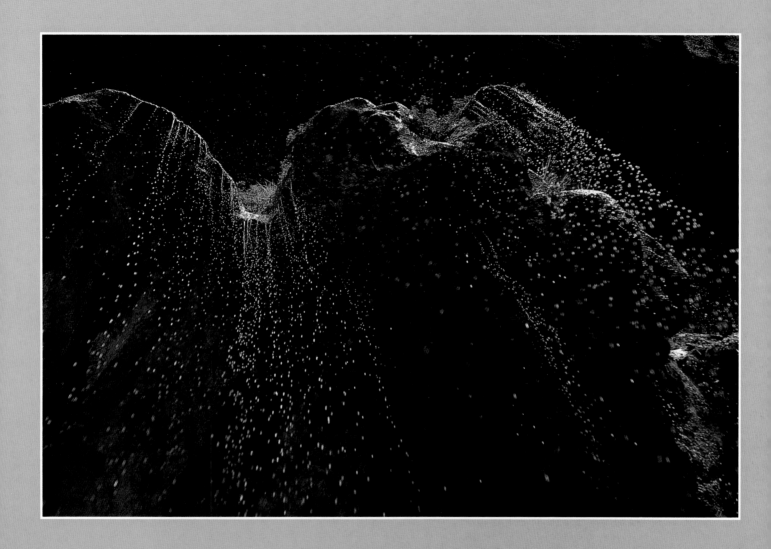

EAST TEMPLE AND MT. MORONI, SUNRISE

SCARLET MONKEYFLOWER AND LEFT FORK OF NORTH CREEK 48

BIGTOOTH MAPLE, AUTUMN

WALL DETAIL AND LEAFING MAPLES, KOLOB CANYON   50

PINE CREEK, WINTER REFLECTIONS

WHITE TUFTED EVENING PRIMROSE AND SANDSTONE

WHITE ARCH, SUNSET

PRICKLY PEAR AND CLIFFS

VIRGIN RIVER AND THE WATCHMAN

Bryce Canyon

SUNRISE FROM BRYCE POINT

This is the land of blue light,
Where sky always touches land.
A place i never have to reach,
For blue light to touch my hand.

Nature's classroom of artwork,
In hoodoos and walls of stone.
A place of silence, a place of peace,
A place you're all alone.

Trees top out of nowhere,
From barren tinted blight.
To grace the side of hoodoo,
And breathe in blue light.

Etched with time and seasons,
Red rock against blue skies.
Change with all of nature's things,
Like when a rain cloud cries.

Light changes constantly
As it moves across the land.
Eye-level floating sky puffs,
Cricket-sifted sand.

Peer through windows, arches and bridges,
Watch ravens soar the sky.
Hoodoos turn to candles,
As the morning sun draws nigh.

A thousand seasons past,
A thousands kinds of life.
A thousand shapes and figures,
In this,
Land of blue light.

This land makes me laugh!

SUNRISE, AGUA CANYON

TUNNEL, PEEK-A-BOO TRAIL

THOR'S HAMMER, WINTER DAY

THOR'S HAMMER, SUNRISE

SUNRISE FROM SUNSET POINT

RAIN SQUALL AT PONDEROSA POINT

BRYCE AMPHITHEATER FROM INSPIRATION POINT

RAINBOW POINT

IN THE QUEEN'S GARDEN

AMPHITHEATER FROM BRYCE POINT

BRYCE AMPHITHEATER WITH PONDEROSA PINE

Nearby Gems

G AFTERNOON, CEDAR BREAKS NATIONAL MONUMENT

SUNSET FROM CHESSMEN RIDGE, CEDAR BREAKS

AFTERNOON FROM THE VISITOR CENTER, CEDAR BREAKS

ARCH, KODACHROME BASIN

ROCK AND CLIFFS, KODACHROME BASIN

CORAL PINK SAND DUNES

STRATIFICATIONS NEAR LEE'S FERRY

This is the Grand Staircase.
Steps of time.
Steps of seasons.
Steps of life.
Steps...everchanging...Steps.

It was here,
      Now it is not.
It is here,
      And is being taken away.
It is under here,
      And is now being revealed.
It is hidden...safely,
      For our grandchildren's,
      grandchildren's, grandchildren.

Like cloud shadows in the night,
You know they are there,
But you seldom see them.

So too, the changes of the Earth.
You know they are happening,
But you seldom see the action.
It is enough ...just to know.

This land makes...me!

STAIRCASE NOTES
by Jim Wilson

THE GRAND STAIRCASE

From a vantage point high above ground level it becomes obvious why geologists refer to this western portion of the 130,000-square-mile Colorado Plateau as the Grand Staircase. The Staircase is a series of angular, uplifted cliffs, retreating to the north as the superimposed rock layers of southern Utah and northern Arizona were eroded. Some of these layers formed at the bottom of ancient seas while others formed on the coastal plains adjacent to the shifting margins of these seas. Others formed as vast windblown sand dunes. These layers were uplifted and are now being eroded by the forces of water, time and gravity. Gazing north from the Kaibab Plateau one sees this series of escarpments resembling giant stair risers while the connecting plateaus appear as great treadways. Travel this giant stairway and your path will ascend from the Kaibab to the Belted or Chocolate Cliffs. Further ascension takes you, in order, up and over the Vermilion, White and Grey Cliffs before reaching the final step, the Pink Cliffs. This region is home to some of the most

PRICKLY PEAR CACTUS

spectacular scenery on earth. Here are Grand Canyon, Zion and Bryce Canyon National Parks, Cedar Breaks National Monument, Coral Pink Sand Dunes and Kodachrome Basin State Parks of Utah and the Bureau of Land Management's Paria/Vermilion Cliffs Wilderness Area. Each preserves a unique landscape as well as providing a piece of a two billion-year-old geologic puzzle. Bryce and Cedar Breaks are eroded into the Pink Cliffs, sedimentary rocks deposited at the bottom of an ancient lake 50 to 60 million years ago. Originally this layer was more than 2,000 feet thick but today measures but 800 to 1,300 feet. Its color comes from iron particles in the rock which oxidize and impart the resulting pink pigment to the entire formation. The Grey Cliffs are of such soft stone that their cliff faces erode faster, and are less perpendicular than those of adjacent formations. Deposited 120 to 135 million years ago, they can be seen at the base of Bryce Canyon as well as along U.S. Highway 89 between Bryce and Zion. The canyons of Zion National Park are carved deep into the White Cliffs. This formation is more than 2,200 feet thick and was deposited from 135 to 165 million years ago. These are the tallest cliffs along the Grand Staircase. Actually tan in color, under direct sunlight they appear white, hence their name. The Vermilion Cliffs, more than 1,000 feet thick, are a brilliant dark red layer deposited 165 to 200 million years ago. They can be seen as vertical cliffs at the base of Zion Canyon as well as towering above Lee's Ferry. The rocks of the Chocolate or Belted Cliffs are 200 to 225 million years old and average 1,800 feet thick. The bottom tread of the Staircase is the 225 million-year-old Kaibab Limestone. However, since most visitors to the region visit Grand Canyon we have included the entire Park in this book. Although it represents the oldest rock of the Staircase, it is the youngest stone to be seen in Grand Canyon National Park. The reason: a deep Colorado River-cut chasm revealing the presence of an additional twenty-one sedimentary and metamorphic rock formations. Following this simplistic overview of the Grand Staircase, the question of elevation differential arises. If Zion is in the middle of the stairway, why is it, at 4,000 feet above sea level, lower than North Rim, at 8,300 feet? The answer is extremely complex and still not fully understood by geologists and earth scientists. Most sedimentary layers, at the time of deposition, were located at or near sea level. Approximately ten million years ago forces from deep within the Earth began uplifting and tilting the flat layers. On the Staircase, each layer retreats to the north. Due to differing compositions and degrees of resistance to fracturing each formation eroded at a different rate, leaving a disparity in elevation. Ecologi-

SEEP AND COLUMBINES

cally the Grand Staircase is as diverse as its geology. It includes the alpine area of Brian Head, north of Cedar Breaks, the subalpine forests of Bryce and North Rim, the ponderosa pine forests of Zion and South Rim, the high desert of the Tonto Plateau and the Sonoran desert environment of the Colorado River level. In addition, many micro-climes are interspersed throughout, each possessing unique characteristics.

THE GRAND CANYON

This chasm is the result of six million years of erosive power unleashed by the Colorado River and its tributaries upon nearly two billion years of sedimentary and metamorphic rock. The landscape, as seen from the rim or experienced from the trail, represents a window into earth's creation. The story these rocks tell is one of intense heat and instability, ancient seas and lakes, powerful uplifts, placid lagoons, Sahara-like deserts and subsequent erosion, all accomplished in a time frame that often appears incomprehensible in human terms. In spite of its seemingly unchanging face, Grand Canyon is indeed dynamic and alive. During our short history it has shown little evidence of change, but there is no doubt that forces which were responsible for creating this park are still at work today. While viewing the vastness of the canyon two questions are often asked by many first time visitors. How was this chasm created and where did all the missing stone go? The Colorado River supplies both answers. Despite its benign appearance, this river and its tributaries are the primary tools of creation. This immense power accomplished the excavation from Marble Canyon to Grand Wash Cliffs in just the last six million years. By geologic standards that is a relatively short period of time. It is difficult to comprehend how all the missing earth could have been removed by what appears to be a relatively insignificant body of water. Yet a stream or river's ability to carry material away increases exponentially during flood stage. It has been calculated that prior to 1963, the average load moved by the Colorado River was nearly 400,000 tons of earth per day. This means that if the load were placed in a series of five-ton dump trucks, it would require 80,000 trucks every 24-hour day to accomplish the same work. Still too great to imagine? Then consider that as you walk the Kaibab Suspension Bridge on the way to Phantom Ranch, at the average rate of two miles per hour, nearly 139 of those dump trucks would have passed beneath your feet. With the completion of the Glen Canyon Dam in 1963, the wild and unpredictable river was harnessed; consequently its ability to move earth was greatly reduced. Today the average load is approximately 80,000 tons per day, about one-fifth of its previous ability. The rock and sand extracted from Grand Canyon now lies downstream behind Hoover Dam and on the

BALANCED ROCK AND PRINCE'S PLUME

floor of the Imperial Valley, creating the massive delta where the river empties into the Gulf of California. The complete story of the creation of the canyon is still not fully understood but the complex process continues while each visitor stands gazing from rim to rim. This is the grand climax of the Grand Staircase, the sum total of all the power nature has released into this geologic region. One can be overwhelmed by a first visit to Grand Canyon and feel comfortable after several visits but few, if any, have ever gained a complete mastery of all that the Park encompasses. Its allure and complexities demand that one return again and again in order to satisfy the thirst for understanding.

ZION NATIONAL PARK

If one had to make the unhappy choice to visit only one area of the Grand Staircase it should be Zion National Park, the one which allows visitors to easily experience the widest diversity of flora and fauna as well as geologic formations. The park's roadways offer easy access to both the canyon bottom along the Virgin River and the rim areas of the high country. In a matter of several hours it is possible to look up and admire the sheer walls cut through the Navajo Sandstone and then, following a short drive, walk atop the crossbedded surface of this same formation. The Virgin River has its beginnings high on the slopes of the Markagunt Plateau where it begins a relentless flow to the Colorado River and Lake Mead. After slicing through the rim of the Kolob Terrace the Virgin drops steeply through a series of sedimentary rocks and carves Zion Canyon. With its spectacular formations and steep walls, it is the scenic heart of this Park. Where the Virgin River cuts through Navajo Sandstone it forms steep, sheer cliffs: a "Narrows" up to two thousand feet deep and barely twenty feet wide. As the river cuts completely through the Navajo and into the softer stones of the Kayenta and Moenave Formations the Narrows end and the portion of Zion Canyon most visitors see begins. Navajo Sandstone is made up of fine quartz grains. They are loosely cemented and yield to erosion yet are rigid enough to support the deep gorge without collapsing. The underlying Kayenta Formation, however, easily washes away and subsequently undercuts the sandstone walls above. Eventually gravity prevails and the walls collapse, widening the canyon. This process becomes evident in the Temple of Sinawava at the Gateway

MAPLE AND CLIFF

to the Narrows. In the American Southwest, water means life. Zion Canyon has been blessed with an abundant, year-round supply of this precious commodity through both the Virgin River and natural springs at the bottom of the Navajo Sandstone. Since the Navajo is quite porous it absorbs water easily and allows it to pass vertically until it reaches the impervious underlying Kayenta Formation. Here the water travels horizontally until it emerges from the canyon walls as seeps and springs. Weeping Rock is a classic example of a seep while Emerald Pools are fed by springs. The presence of these springs creates a paradox of lush riparian habitats co-existing with semi-arid desert habitats. Columbines bloom proximal to prickly pear, and the songs of ouzels and canyon wrens can be heard simultaneously. Passing through the Zion-Mt. Carmel Tunnel brings you into Zion's high country. At the east end of this 6,607-foot tunnel a short trail leads to Canyon Overlook, with its spectacular view down Pine Creek to Towers of the Virgin. The Zion-Mt. Carmel Highway cuts through a land of crossbedded sandstone, mounds of rock which are the top of the Navajo Sandstone. They are the remnants of windblown dunes which were frozen in place 150 million years ago in an ancient Sahara-like desert. Atop the Navajo there is little soil, consequently most water runs off rapidly. With a little effort one can locate and explore numerous narrow "slots" formed by these watercourses. There is much about Zion that makes it special. It is rich in human history and fascinating to geologists but, above all, it is alive and constantly changing. Long time fans of Zion National Park have found it necessary to return time after time, in order to gain a deeper knowledge and understanding of its appeal.

BRYCE CANYON NATIONAL PARK
High atop the Paunsaugunt Plateau, home to subalpine

forests reminiscent of a high mountain range, lies the youngest sedimentary layer visible today on the Grand Staircase. This layer, the Claron Formation, was laid down approximately 50 to 60 million years ago as lime, mud and silt from shallow lakes and rivers. By the time this silty, impure limestone, long since transformed to stone, reached the surface through erosion, the pressure of uplift had left them fractured. Such fracturing renders soft limestones ripe for excavation. Averaging 8,000 feet above sea level, Bryce is subjected to heavy winter precipitation, usually half snow and half rain. Winter's freeze-expansion-thaw process combined with heavy summer thundershowers contributes greatly to Bryce's rapid erosion. From the rim, spread out before you is the magic of that erosion, forms of such intense colors and whimsical shapes that they inspired names such as Fairyland, Silent City, Thor's Hammer and Sinking Ship. Below the rim one can become intimate with these

ROCK AND WATER

columns, castles, arches and windows. Throughout the day, changing light capriciously paints the formations in shades of red, pink and umber lending an air of enchantment to the amphitheater. It is easy to become so enchanted that one overlooks an important attribute of Bryce, its magnificent view. On a clear day you can see more than one hundred miles. To the east lies the 11,000-foot Aquarius Plateau and the rounded dome of Navajo Mountain. To the south, looking down the Grand Staircase, lies the Paria Plateau and the state of Arizona.

NEARBY SCENIC GEMS:

CEDAR BREAKS NATIONAL MONUMENT. There are numerous similarities between Bryce Canyon and Cedar Breaks. Both are great amphitheaters carved into the Claron Formation possessing fascinating erosional forms which change color with the changing light. Bryce is etched into the east face of the Paunsaugunt Plateau while Cedar Breaks is carved into the west-facing side of the Markagunt Plateau and, at 10,000 feet in elevation, is considerably higher than Bryce. Behind the "breaks" is a lush subalpine spruce-fir forest. In the summer season, fragrant wildflower-rich meadows bloom in profusion. Beginning in late June and continuing through mid-August this area flaunts its natural flair for life with an annual show of wildflowers. At various times of the season one can find mountain bluebell, Indian paintbrush, fleabane, beardtongue, larkspur, lupine, penstemon and columbine, all uncommon in other lower-elevation parks of the Grand Staircase.

Often overlooked by destination bound visitors, this hoodoo-rich scenic area offers easy access to formations eroded from the same 50 to 60 million-year-old Claron Formation found in nearby Bryce Canyon National Park. To help visitors better understand the forces which created this area, the National Forest Service operates a visitor center on Utah State Highway 12, midway through the canyon.

KODACHROME BASIN STATE PARK. This Utah State Park preserves a unique, rich red landscape that scientists speculate resembled, in earlier times, what Yellowstone National Park is today, an area of open springs and geysers. These have long since filled with sediment and solidified into the spires, or sand pipes which were left exposed when the softer surrounding Entrada Formation was eroded away. Found solely in Kodachrome Basin, sixty-seven have been identified ranging in height from 6 to 166 feet.

CORAL PINK SAND DUNES STATE PARK. This Utah State Park is of interest to visitors and scientists alike for it offers an evolving study in how the Navajo Sandstone layer was formed. The dunes found here were formed from loose sand grains blown into place by hot swirling southerly winds. The unique color of the dunes is the result of a high concentration of iron oxides in the sand.

PIPE SPRING NATIONAL MONUMENT. In 1869, following the cessation of the Navajo Indian raids, Mormon settlers re-established this former home of James Whitmore. They enclosed the natural spring inside Winsor Castle, a rock fort named for Anson Winsor. It soon became a

PAINTBRUSH AND BLUEBELLS

thriving agricultural outpost, flourishing throughout the 1870's and 1880's. Eventually the great cooperative herds of cattle raised here overgrazed the surrounding pasture and fragile desert, bringing about their own decline. In 1923 the National Park Service acquired the Castle and closely surrounding property, in order to preserve its unique history. Today the National Park Service maintains the land and works the farm as its settlers did. The orchards still produce a bounty of fruit, and interpreters manufacture cheese and bake breads and rolls as in olden days.

LEE'S FERRY, VERMILION CLIFFS AREA. Lee's Ferry lies on the break between Glen and Marble Canyons at the confluence of the Paria and Colorado Rivers . A natural corridor between Arizona and Utah, it figured prominently in the exploration and settlement of the surrounding canyon country. In 1871 John D. Lee established a ferry service across the Colorado River at this location. Due to Navajo unrest a stone fort was built, becoming a focal point for settlers and miners working the canyon country. In addition to being a traditional starting point for Grand Canyon river trips, it is also a popular beginning or ending point for backpackers exploring the Paria/Vermilion Cliffs Wilderness Area.

PHOTOGRAPHIC CREDITS

Russ Bishop: 70.
Chris Cruz: 23.
Russ Finley: 60.
Frank Hotz: 71.
Leland Howard/ F-Stock: 68.
George H.H. Huey: Cover (center) ,30,52, 54,55,
57,77,88.
Gary Ladd: 8,9,24.
William Neill: 11,20,42.
Jeff Nicholas: Cover (left),6,10,12,17,21,22,28,31,
32,35,36,39,40,41,45,47,51,56,58,
61,62,67,69,73,74,78,79,81,83,84,
86,87,92,94,95.
Jeff Nixon: 49.
Pat O'Hara: 26.
Randall K. Roberts: 37.
John Telford: 33,50.
Tom Till: 15,18,27.
Larry Ulrich: 13,14,48,64,76.
Jim Wilson: Cover (right),16,19,25,34,38,43,44,46
53,63,65,66,72,75,80,82,85,90,91,93.
Copyrights to all photographs remain with the artist.

CREDITS

Poetic Text by Lynn Wilson
Introduction by Jeff Nicholas
Staircase Notes by Jim Wilson
Edited by Ardeth Huntington

Graphic Design by Jeff Nicholas

Back Cover Illustration by Jeff Nicholas

Layout and graphic design performed on a Macintosh® SE utilizing Aldus PageMaker® and Microsoft Word®. All texts set in Palatino and Optima Typefaces by MacinType, Fresno, Ca. Color separations and printing coordinated by Interprint, Petaluma, Ca.